Poems of
Rudyard
Kipling

POEMS OF
RUDYARD
KIPLING

WITH ILLUSTRATIONS BY
W. HEATH ROBINSON

GRAMERCY BOOKS

NEW YORK · AVENEL

This edition is published by Gramercy Books,
distributed by Random House Value Publishing, Inc.
40 Engelhard Avenue
Avenel, New Jersey 07001

Random House
New York • Toronto • London • Sydney • Auckland

Designed by Kathryn W. Plosica

Printed and bound in Singapore

Library of Congress Cataloging-in-Publication Data
Kipling, Rudyard, 1865-1936.
[Poems. Selections]
Poems of Rudyard Kipling.
p. cm.
ISBN 0-517-12276-6
I. Title.
PR4852 1995b
821'.8—dc20   94-39819
                                                        CIP

8 7 6 5 4 3 2 1

Contents

Introduction

Rudyard Kipling was, for many years, one of the most popular poets who ever lived. His huge audience was attracted by the freshness of his subjects, his ability to capture the emotions and energy of the speakers, and his mastery of the rhythms of verse.

Kipling was born in Bombay, to English parents, on December 30, 1865. As was the custom, at the age of six he was sent "home" to England for his education, but those early years had imbued him with a love of India that influenced his work throughout his career.

He returned to India eleven years later. His father, John Lockwood Kipling, an artist of considerable talent, was the curator of the museum in Lahore. Young Kipling went to work as the subeditor of the Lahore *Civil and Military Gazette* and spent any free time writing short stories and some poetry. ("The Files" was written during this period.)

When, a few years later, he published *Plain Tales from the Hills*—stories that explored the psychological and moral conflicts of Englishmen and their wives living in the midst of a subject people —his talent as a master of fiction was established in India and in England. In 1887, Kipling had left Lahore to travel through India, China, Japan, and America. Two years later, when he arrived in England, he found that he was famous.

In 1892, his *Barrack Room Ballads*, many of which first appeared in the *National Observer*, were published. These vigorous verses won him prominence as a poet, and a second fame far wider

than he had attained as a storyteller. That same year Kipling married an American, Caroline Starr Balestier, and they lived for five years in Brattleboro, Vermont, before settling in England.

In his poems Kipling often drew upon the Indian scene, usually through the eyes and Cockney accents of ordinary British soldiers who had been sent out from England to protect the country and fight invaders of the northwest frontier. Using lots of army slang, these soldiers described, often with bewilderment or great sadness, their experiences and events in which they had participated. In some of these poems the speakers' attitudes toward Indians will strike modern readers as offensive. They accurately record, however, the way British soldiers in the late nineteenth century viewed the strange lands in which they served.

A vigorous and unconventional poet, as well as one of the rare masters of the art of the short story, Rudyard Kipling had, by the beginning of the twentieth century, won a prominent place in the pantheon of great writers. In 1907 he was awarded the Nobel Prize for literature, the first English author to receive the prize. He died in London on January 18, 1936, leaving a legacy of poems, stories, and novels to be enjoyed by generations to come.

This collection includes many poems from the *Barrack Room Ballads*—"Gunga Din," "Danny Deever," "The Ballad of East and West," and "The Last of the Light Brigade" among them—the universally popular "If," and "Recessional," originally published in *The Times* on July 17, 1897, on the occasion of Queen Victoria's second jubilee.

The illustrations of W. Heath Robinson, a contemporary of Kipling's, evoke the vitality of the verses.

GAIL HARVEY

New York
1995

If

If you can keep your head when all about you
　　Are losing theirs and blaming it on you;
If you can trust yourself when all men doubt
　　　you,
　　But make allowance for their doubting too;
If you can wait and not be tired by waiting,
　　Or, being lied about, don't deal in lies,
Or, being hated, don't give way to hating,
　　And yet don't look too good, nor talk too
　　　wise;

If you can dream—and not make dreams your
　　　master;
　　If you can think—and not make thoughts
　　　your aim;
If you can meet with triumph and disaster
　　And treat those two impostors just the
　　　same;
If you can bear to hear the truth you've
　　　spoken
　　Twisted by knaves to make a trap for fools,
Or watch the things you gave your life to
　　　broken,
　　And stoop and build 'em up with wornout
　　　tools;

If you can make one heap of all your
    winnings
  And risk it on one turn of pitch-and-toss,
And lose, and start again at your beginnings
  And never breathe a word about your loss;
If you can force your heart and nerve and
    sinew
  To serve your turn long after they are gone,
And so hold on when there is nothing in you
  Except the Will which says to them: "Hold
    on";

If you can talk with crowds and keep your
    virtue,
  Or walk with kings—nor lose the common
    touch;
If neither foes nor loving friends can hurt
    you;
  If all men count with you, but none too
    much;
If you can fill the unforgiving minute
  With sixty seconds' worth of distance run—
Yours is the Earth and everything that's in it,
  And—which is more—you'll be a Man, my
    son!

The Ballad of East and West

Oh, East is East, and West is West, and never the twain shall
    meet,
Till Earth and Sky stand presently at God's great Judgment Seat;
But there is neither East nor West, Border, nor Breed, nor Birth,
When two strong men stand face to face, tho' they come from the
    ends of the earth!

Kamal is out with twenty men to raise the borderside,
And he has lifted the Colonel's mare that is the Colonel's pride:
He has lifted her out of the stable door between the dawn and
    the day,
And turned the calkins upon her feet, and ridden her far away.
Then up and spoke the Colonel's son that led a troop of the
    Guides:
"Is there never a man of all my men can say where Kamal
    hides?"
Then up and spoke Mohammed Khan, the son of the Ressaldar:
"If ye know the track of the morning mist, ye know where his
    pickets are.
"At dusk he harries the Abazai—at dawn he is into Bonair,
"But he must go by Fort Bukloh to his own place to fare,
"So if ye gallop to Fort Bukloh as fast as a bird can fly,
"By the favor of God ye may cut him off ere he win to the
    Tongue of Jagai.

"But if he be past the Tongue of Jagai, right swiftly turn ye
then,

"For the length and the breadth of that grisly plain is sown with
Kamal's men.

"There is rock to the left, and rock to the right, and low lean
thorn between,

"And ye may hear a breech bolt snick where never a man is
seen."

The Colonel's son has taken a horse, and a raw rough dun was
he,

With the mouth of a bell and the heart of Hell and the head of a
gallows tree.

The Colonel's son to the Fort has won, they bid him stay to
eat—

Who rides at the tail of a border thief, he sits not long at his
meat.

He's up and away from Fort Bukloh as fast as he can fly,

Till he was aware of his father's mare in the gut of the Tongue of
Jagai,

Till he was aware of his father's mare with Kamal upon her
back,

And when he could spy the white of her eye, he made the pistol
crack.

He has fired once, he has fired twice, but the whistling ball went
wide.

"Ye shoot like a soldier," Kamal said. "Show now if ye can ride."

It's up and over the Tongue of Jagai, as blown dust devils go,

The dun he fled like a stag of ten, but the mare like a barren
doe.

The dun he leaned against the bit and slugged his head above,
But the red mare played with the snaffle bars, as a maiden
    plays with a glove.
There was rock to the left and rock to the right, and low lean
    thorn between,
And thrice he heard a breech bolt snick tho' never a man was
    seen.
They have ridden the low moon out of the sky, their hoofs drum
    up the dawn,
The dun he went like a wounded bull, but the mare like a
    new-roused fawn.
The dun he fell at a watercourse—in a woeful heap fell he,
And Kamal has turned the red mare back, and pulled the rider
    free.
He has knocked the pistol out of his hand—small room was
    there to strive,
" 'Twas only by favor of mine," quoth he, "ye rode so long alive:
"There was not a rock for twenty mile, there was not a clump of
    tree,
"But covered a man of my own men with his rifle cocked on his
    knee.
"If I had raised my bridle-hand, as I have held it low,
"The little jackals that flee so fast were feasting all in a row:
"If I had bowed my head on my breast, as I have held it high,
"The kite that whistles above us now were gorged till she could
    not fly."
Lightly answered the Colonel's son: "Do good to bird and beast,
"But count who come for the broken meats before thou makest
    a feast.
"If there should follow a thousand swords to carry my bones
    away,

"Belike the price of a jackal's meal were more than a thief could
	pay.
"They will feed their horse on the standing crop, their men on
	the garnered grain,
"The thatch of the byres will serve their fires when all the cattle
	are slain.
"But if thou thinkest the price be fair,—thy brethren wait to
	sup,
"The hound is kin to the jackal-spawn,—howl, dog, and call
	them up!
"And if thou thinkest the price be high, in steer and gear and
	stack,
"Give me my father's mare again, and I'll fight my own way
	back!"
Kamal has gripped him by the hand and set him upon his feet.
"No talk shall be of dogs," said he, "when wolf and gray wolf
	meet.
"May I eat dirt if thou hast hurt of me in deed or breath;
"What dam of lances brought thee forth to jest at the dawn with
	Death?"
Lightly answered the Colonel's son: "I hold by the blood of my
	clan:
"Take up the mare for my father's gift—by God, she has carried
	a man!"
The red mare ran to the Colonel's son, and muzzled against his
	breast;
"We be two strong men," said Kamal then, "but she loveth the
	younger best.
"So she shall go with a lifter's dower, my turquoise-studded
	rein,
"My broidered saddle and saddle-cloth, and silver stirrups
	twain."

The Colonel's son a pistol drew, and held it muzzle-end,
"Ye have take the one from a foe," said he; "will ye take the mate
    from a friend?"
"A gift for a gift," said Kamal straight; "a limb for the risk of a
    limb.
"Thy father has sent his son to me, I'll send my son to him!"
With that he whistled his only son, that dropped from a
    mountain crest—
He trod the ling like a buck in spring, and he looked like a lance
    in rest.
"Now here is thy master," Kamal said, "who leads a troop of the
    Guides,
"And thou must ride at his left side as shield on shoulder rides.
"Till Death or I cut loose the tie, at camp and board and bed,
"Thy life is his—thy fate it is to guard him with thy head.
"So, thou must eat the white Queen's meat, and all her foes are
    thine,
"And thou must harry thy father's hold for the peace of the
    borderline,
"And thou must make a trooper tough and hack thy way to
    power—
"Belike they will raise thee to Ressaldar when I am hanged in
    Peshawar."

They have looked each other between the eyes, and there they
    found no fault,
They have taken the Oath of the Brother-in-Blood on leavened
    bread and salt:
They have taken the Oath of the Brother-in-Blood on fire and
    fresh-cut sod,
On the hilt and the haft of the Khyber knife, and the
    Wondrous Names of God.

The Colonel's son he rides the mare and Kamal's boy the dun,
And two have come back to Fort Bukloh where there went forth
    but one.
And when they drew to the Quarter-Guard, full twenty swords
    flew clear—
There was not a man but carried his feud with the blood of the
    mountaineer.
"Ha' done! ha' done!" said the Colonel's son. "Put up the steel at
    your sides!
"Last night ye had struck at a border thief—tonight 'tis a man of
    the Guides!"

*Oh, East is East, and West is West, and never the twain shall
    meet,*
Till Earth and Sky stand presently at God's great Judgment Seat;
But there is neither East nor West, Border, nor Breed, nor Birth,
*When two strong men stand face to face, tho' they come from the
    ends of the earth!*

L'Envoi

The smoke upon your Altar dies,
    The flowers decay,
The Goddess of your sacrifice
    Has flown away.
What profit then to sing or slay
The sacrifice from day to day?

"We know the Shrine is void," they said,
    "The Goddess flown—
"Yet wreaths are on the altar laid—
    "The Altar-Stone
"Is black with fumes of sacrifice,
"Albeit She has fled our eyes.

"For, it may be, if still we sing
    "And tend the Shrine,
"Some Deity on wandering wing
    "May there incline;
"And, finding all in order meet,
"Stay while we worship at Her feet."

Evarra and His Gods

Read here:
This is the story of Evarra—man—
Maker of Gods in lands beyond the sea.
  Because the city gave him of her gold,
  Because the caravans brought turquoises,
  Because his life was sheltered by the King,
  So that no man should maim him, none should steal,
  Or break his rest with babble in the streets
  When he was weary after toil, he made
  An image of his God in gold and pearl,
  With turquoise diadem and human eyes,
  A wonder in the sunshine, known afar,
  And worshipped by the King; but, drunk with pride,
  Because the city bowed to him for God,
  He wrote above the shrine: *"Thus Gods are made,*
  "And whoso makes them otherwise shall die."
  And all the city praised him. . . . Then he died.

Read here the story of Evarra—man—
Maker of Gods in lands beyond the sea.
  Because the city had no wealth to give,
  Because the caravans were spoiled afar,
  Because his life was threatened by the King,
  So that all men despised him in the streets,

He hewed the living rock, with sweat and tears,
And reared a God against the morning-gold,
A terror in the sunshine, seen afar,
And worshipped by the King; but, drunk with pride,
Because the city fawned to bring him back,
He carved upon the plinth: *"Thus Gods are made,*
"And whoso makes them otherwise shall die."
And all the people praised him. . . . Then he died.

Read here the story of Evarra—man—
Maker of Gods in lands beyond the sea.
Because he lived among a simple folk,
Because his village was between the hills,
Because he smeared his cheeks with blood of ewes,
He cut an idol from a fallen pine,
Smeared blood upon its cheeks, and wedged a shell
Above its brows for eyes, and gave it hair
Of trailing moss, and plaited straw for crown.
And all the village praised him for this craft,
And brought him butter, honey, milk, and curds.
Wherefore, because the shoutings drove him mad,
He scratched upon that log: *"Thus Gods are made,*
"And whoso makes them otherwise shall die."
And all the people praised him. . . . Then he died.

Read here the story of Evarra—man—
Maker of Gods in lands beyond the sea.
Because his God decreed one clot of blood
Should swerve one hair's breadth from the pulse's path,
And chafe his brain, Evarra mowed alone,
Rag-wrapped, among the cattle in the fields,
Counting his fingers, jesting with the trees,
And mocking at the mist, until his God
Drove him to labor. Out of dung and horns

Dropped in the mire he made a monstrous God,
Uncleanly, shapeless, crowned with plantain tufts,
And when the cattle lowed at twilight time,
He dreamed it was the clamor of lost crowds,
And howled among the beasts: *"Thus Gods are made,
"And whoso makes them otherwise shall die."*
Thereat the cattle bellowed. . . . Then he died.

Yet at the last he came to Paradise,
And found his own four Gods, and that he wrote;
And marveled, being very near to God,
What oaf on earth had made his toil God's law,
Till God said mocking: "Mock not. These be thine."
Then cried Evarra: "I have sinned!"—"Not so.
"If thou hadst written otherwise, thy Gods
"Had rested in the mountain and the mine,
"And I were poorer by four wondrous Gods,
"And thy more wondrous law, Evarra. Thine,
"Servant of shouting crowds and lowing kine!"

Thereat, with laughing mouth, but tear-wet eyes,
Evarra cast his Gods from Paradise.

This is the story of Evarra—man—
Maker of Gods in lands beyond the sea.

The Last of the Light Brigade

There were thirty million English who talked of England's
    might,
There were twenty broken troopers who lacked a bed for
    the night.
They had neither food nor money, they had neither service
    nor trade;
They were only shiftless soldiers, the last of the Light
    Brigade.

They felt that life was fleeting; they knew not that art was
    long,
That though they were dying of famine, they lived in
    deathless song.
They asked for a little money to keep the wolf from the
    door;
And the thirty million English sent twenty pounds and
    four!

They laid their heads together that were scarred and lined
    and gray;
Keen were the Russian sabers, but want was keener than
    they;
And an old Troop-Sergeant muttered, "Let us go to the man
    who writes
The things on Balaclava the kiddies at school recites."

They went without bands or colors, a regiment ten-file
strong,
To look for the Master-singer who had crowned them all
in his song;
And, waiting his servant's order, by the garden gate they
stayed,
A desolate little cluster, the last of the Light Brigade.

They stove to stand to attention, to straighten the toil-bowed
back;
They drilled on an empty stomach, the loose-knit files fell
slack;
With stooping of weary shoulders, in garments tattered and
frayed,
They shambled into his presence, the last of the Light
Brigade.

The old Troop-Sergeant was spokesman, and "Beggin' your
pardon," he said,
"You wrote o' the Light Brigade, sir. Here's all that isn't
dead.
An' it's all come true what you wrote, sir, regardin' the
mouth of hell;
For we're all of us nigh to the workhouse, an' we thought
we'd call an' tell.

No, thank you, we don't want food, sir; but couldn't you
take an' write
A sort of 'to be continued' and 'see next page' o' the fight?
We think that someone has blundered, an' couldn't you tell
'em how?

You wrote we were heroes once, sir. Please, write we are
    starving now."

The poor little army departed, limping and lean and
    forlorn.
And the heart of the Master-singer grew hot with "the acorn
    of scorn."
And he wrote for them wonderful verses that swept the land
    like flame,
Till the fatted souls of the English were scourged with the
    thing called Shame.

O thirty million English that babble of England's might,
Behold there are twenty heroes who lack their food
    tonight;
Our children's children are lisping to "honor the charge
    they made—"
And we leave to the streets and the workhouse the charge
    of the Light Brigade!

Gunga Din

You may talk o' gin and beer
When you're quartered safe out 'ere,
An' you're sent to penny-fights an' Aldershot it;
But when it comes to slaughter
You will do your work on water,
An' you'll lick the bloomin' boots of 'im that's got it.
Now in Injia's sunny clime,
Where I used to spend my time
A-servin' of 'Er Majesty the Queen,
Of all them blackfaced crew
The finest man I knew
Was our regimental bhisti, Gunga Din.
        He was "Din! Din! Din!
    "You limpin' lump o' brick-dust, Gunga Din!
        "Hi! slippery *hitherao!*
        "Water, get it! *Panee lao!**
    "You squidgy-nosed old idol, Gunga Din."

The uniform 'e wore
Was nothin' much before,
An' rather less than 'arf o' that be'ind,
For a piece o' twisty rag
An' a goatskin water bag
Was all the field equipment 'e could find.
When the sweatin' troop train lay
In a sidin' through the day,

---

* Bring water quickly!

29

Where the 'eat would make your bloomin' eyebrows crawl,
We shouted "Harry By!"[1]
Till our throats were bricky-dry,
Then we wopped 'im cause 'e couldn't serve us all.
   It was "Din! Din! Din!
  "You 'eathen, where the mischief 'ave you been?
   "You put some *juldee*[2] in it
   "Or I'll *marrow*[3] you this minute
  "If you don't fill up my helmet, Gunga Din!"

'E would dot an' carry one
Till the longest day was done;
An' 'e didn't seem to know the use o' fear.
If we charged or broke or cut,
You could bet your bloomin' nut,
'E'd be waitin' fifty paces right flank rear.
With 'is mussick[4] on 'is back,
'E would skip with our attack,
An' watch us till the bugles made "Retire,"
An' for all 'is dirty 'ide
'E was white, clear white, inside
When 'e went to tend the wounded under fire!
   It was "Din! Din! Din!"
  With the bullets kickin' dust spots on the green
   When the cartridges ran out,
   You could hear the front-ranks shout,
  "Hi! ammunition-mules an' Gunga Din!"

I sha'n't forgit the night
When I dropped be'ind the fight
With a bullet where my belt-plate should 'a' been.

[1] Mr. Atkins's attempt at saying, "O Brother."
[2] Speed
[3] Hit you.
[4] Waterskin

I was chokin' mad with thirst,
An' the man that spied me first
Was our good old grinnin', gruntin' Gunga Din.
'E lifted up my 'ead,
An' he plugged me where I bled,
An' 'e guv me 'arf-a-pint o' water-green:
It was crawlin' and it stunk,
But of all the drinks I've drunk,
I'm gratefullest to one from Gunga Din.
        It was "Din! Din! Din!
          " 'Ere's a beggar with a bullet through 'is spleen;
              " 'E's chawin' up the ground,
             "An' 'e's kickin' all around:
         "For Gawd's sake git the water, Gunga Din!"

'E carried me away
To where a dooli lay,
An' a bullet come an' drilled the beggar clean.
'E put me safe inside,
An' just before 'e died,
"I 'ope you liked your drink," sez Gunga Din.
So I'll meet 'im later on
At the place where 'e is gone—
Where it's always double drill and no canteen;
'E'll be squattin' on the coals
Givin' drink to poor damned souls,
An' I'll get a swig in hell from Gunga Din!
          Yes, Din! Din! Din!
       You Lazarushian-leather Gunga Din!
          Though I've belted you and flayed you,
           By the livin' Gawd that made you,
        You're a better man than I am, Gunga Din!

Tommy

I went into a public 'ouse to get a pint o' beer,
The publican 'e up an' sez, "We serve no red-coats here."
The girls be'ind the bar they laughed an' giggled fit to die,
I outs into the street again an' to myself sez I:
    O it's Tommy this, an' Tommy that, an' "Tommy, go
        away";
    But it's "Thank you, Mister Atkins," when the band
        begins to play,
    The band begins to play, my boys, the band begins to
        play,
    O it's "Thank you, Mister Atkins," when the band begins
        to play.

I went into a theater as sober as could be,
They gave a drunk civilian room, but 'adn't none for me;
They sent me to the gallery or round the music 'alls,
But when it comes to fightin', Lord! they'll shove me in the
    stalls!
    For it's Tommy this, an' Tommy that, an' "Tommy, wait
        outside";
    But it's "Special train for Atkins" when the trooper's on
        the tide,
    The troopship's on the tide, my boys, the troopship's on
        the tide,
    O it's "Special train for Atkins" when the trooper's on
        the tide.

Yes, makin' mock o' uniforms that guard you while you
    sleep
Is cheaper than them uniforms, an' they're starvation
    cheap;
An' hustlin' drunken soldiers when they're goin' large a bit
Is five times better business than paradin' in full kit.
    Then it's Tommy this, an' Tommy that, an' "Tommy,
        'ow's yer soul?"
    But it's "Thin red line of 'eroes" when the drums begin
        to roll,
    The drums begin to roll, my boys, the drums begin to
        roll,
    O it's "Thin red line of 'eroes" when the drums begin
        to roll.

We aren't no thin red 'eroes, nor we aren't no blackguards
    too,
But single men in barricks, most remarkable like you;
An' if sometimes our conduck isn't all your fancy paints,
Why, single men in barricks don't grow into plaster saints;
    While it's Tommy this, an' Tommy that, an' "Tommy,
        fall be'ind,"
    But it's "Please to walk in front, sir," when there's trouble
        in the wind,
    There's trouble in the wind, my boys, there's trouble in
        the wind,
    O it's "Please to walk in front, sir," when there's trouble
        in the wind.

You talk o' better food for us, an' schools, an' fires, an' all:
We'll wait for extry rations if you treat us rational.
Don't mess about the cook-room slops, but prove it to our
    face
The Widow's Uniform is not the soldier-man's disgrace.
For it's Tommy this, an' Tommy that, an' "Chuck him
    out, the brute!"
But it's "Savior of 'is country" when the guns begin to
    shoot;
An' it's Tommy this, an' Tommy that, an' anything you
    please;
An' Tommy ain't a bloomin' fool—you bet that Tommy
    sees!

Danny Deever

"What are the bugles blowin' for?" said Files-on-Parade.
"To turn you out, to turn you out," the Color-Sergeant said.
"What makes you look so white, so white?" said Files-on-
    Parade.
"I'm dreadin' what I've got to watch," the Color-Sergeant
    said.
  For they're hangin' Danny Deever, you can hear the
      Dead March play,
  The regiment's in 'ollow square—they're hangin' him today;
  They've taken of his buttons off an' cut his stripes away,
  An' they're hangin' Danny Deever in the mornin'.

"What makes the rear-rank breathe so 'ard?" said Files-on
    -Parade.
"It's bitter cold, it's bitter cold," the Color-Sergeant said.
"What makes that front-rank man fall down?" says Files-
    on-Parade.
"A touch o' sun, a touch o' sun," the Color-Sergeant said.
  They are hangin' Danny Deever, they are marchin' of 'im
      round,
  They 'ave 'alted Danny Deever by 'is coffin on the ground;
  An' 'e'll swing in 'arf a minute for a sneakin' shootin'
      hound—
  O they're hangin' Danny Deever in the mornin'!

" 'Is cot was right-'and cot to mine," said Files-on-Parade.
" 'E's sleepin' out an' far tonight," the Color-Sergeant said.
"I've drunk 'is beer a score o' times," said Files-on-Parade.
" 'E's drinkin' bitter beer alone," the Color-Sergeant said.
   They are hangin' Danny Deever, you must mark 'im to
        'is place,
     For 'e shot a comrade sleepin'—you must look 'im in the
        face;
     Nine 'undred of 'is county an' the regiment's disgrace,
     While they're hangin' Danny Deever in the mornin'.

"What's that so black agin the sun?" said Files-on-Parade.
"It's Danny fightin' 'ard for life," the Color-Sergeant said.
"What's that that whimpers over'ead?" said Files-on-Parade.
"It's Danny's soul that's passing now," the Color-Sergeant
    said.
   For they're done with Danny Deever, you can 'ear the
       quickstep play,
     The regiment's in column, an' they're marchin' us away;
     Ho! the young recruits are shakin', an' they'll want their
       beer today,
     After hangin' Danny Deever in the mornin'.

The Widow at Windsor

'Ave you 'eard o' the Widow at Windsor
  With a hairy gold crown on 'er 'ead?
She 'as ships on the foam—she 'as millions at 'ome,
  An' she pays us poor beggars in red.
    (Ow, poor beggars in red!)
There's 'er nick on the cavalry 'orses,
  There's 'er mark on the medical stores—
An' 'er troopers you'll find with a fair wind be'ind
  That takes us to various wars.
    (Poor beggars!—barbarious wars!)
    Then 'ere's to the Widow at Windsor,
      An' 'ere's to the stores an' the guns,
    The men an' the 'orses what makes up the forces
      O' Missis Victorier's sons.
    (Poor beggars! Victorier's sons!)

Walk wide o' the Widow at Windsor,
  For 'alf o' Creation she owns:
We 'ave bought 'er the same with the sword an' the flame,
  An' we've salted it down with our bones.
    (Poor beggars!—it's blue with our bones!)
Hands off o' the sons o' the Widow,
  Hands off o' the goods in 'er shop,
For the Kings must come down an' the Emperors frown
  When the Widow at Windsor says "Stop!"
    (Poor beggars!—we're sent to say "Stop!")

Then 'ere's to the Lodge o' the Widow,
    From the Pole to the Tropics it runs—
To the Lodge that we tile with the rank an' the file,
    An' open in form with the guns.
        (Poor beggars!—it's always they guns!)

We 'ave 'eard o' the Widow at Windsor,
    It's safest to let 'er alone:
For 'er sentries we stand by the sea an' the land
    Wherever the bugles are blown.
        (Poor beggars!—an' don't we get blown!)
Take 'old o' the Wings o' the Mornin',
    An' flop round the earth till you're dead;
But you won't get away from the tune that they play
    To the bloomin' old Rag over'ead.
        (Poor beggars!—it's 'ot over'ead!)
    Then 'ere's to the sons o' the Widow,
        Wherever, 'owever they roam.
    'Ere's all they desire, an' if they require
        A speedy return to their 'ome.
    (Poor beggars!—they'll never see 'ome!)

Mandalay

By the old Moulmein Pagoda, lookin' eastward to the sea,
There's a Burma girl a-settin', and I know she thinks o' me;
For the wind is in the palm trees, and the temple bells they
    say:
"Come you back, you British soldier; come you back to
    Mandalay!"
      Come you back to Mandalay,
      Where the old flotilla lay:
      Can't you 'ear their paddles chunkin' from
        Rangoon to Mandalay?
      On the road to Mandalay,
      Where the flyin' fishes play,
      An' the dawn comes up like thunder outer
        China 'crost the bay!

'Er petticoat was yaller an' 'er little cap was green,
An' 'er name was Supi-yaw-lat—jes' the same as Theebaw's
    Queen,
An' I seed her first a-smokin' of a whackin' white cheroot,
An' a-wastin' Christian kisses on an 'eathen idol's foot:
      Bloomin' idol made o' mud—
      Wot they call the Great Gawd Budd—
      Plucky lot she cared for idols when I kissed 'er
        where she stud!
      On the road to Mandalay . . .

40

When the mist was on the rice fields an' the sun was
    droppin' slow,
She'd get 'er little banjo an' she'd sing "*Kulla-lo-lo!*"
With 'er arm upon my shoulder an' 'er cheek agin my
    cheek
We useter watch the steamers an' the *hathis* pilin' teak.
        Elephints a-pilin' teak
        In the sludgy, squdgy creek,
        Where the silence 'ung that 'eavy you was 'arf
            afraid to speak!
        On the road to Mandalay . . .

But that's all shove be'ind me—long ago an' fur away,
An' there ain't no 'busses runnin' from the Bank to
    Mandalay;
An' I'm learnin' 'ere in London what the ten-year soldier
    tells:
"If you've 'eard the East a-callin', you won't never 'eed
    naught else."
        No! you won't 'eed nothin' else
        But them spicy garlic smells,
        An' the sunshine an' the palm trees an' the
            tinkly temple bells;
        On the road to Mandalay . . .

I am sick o' wastin' leather on these gritty pavin' stones,
An' the blasted Henglish drizzle wakes the fever in my
    bones;
Tho' I walks with fifty 'ousemaids outer Chelsea to the
    Strand,
An' they talks a lot o' lovin', but wot do they understand?
        Beefy face an' grubby 'and—
        Law! wot do they understand?

I've a neater, sweeter maiden in a cleaner, greener
    land!
On the road to Mandalay . . .

Ship me somewheres east of Suez, where the best is like
    the worst,
Where there aren't no Ten Commandments an' a man can
    raise a thirst;
For the temple-bells are callin', an' it's there that I would
    be—
By the old Moulmein Pagoda, looking lazy at the sea;
    On the road to Mandalay,
    Where the old flotilla lay,
    With our sick beneath the awnings when we went to
        Mandalay!
    O the road to Mandalay,
    Where the flyin' fishes play,
    An' the dawn comes up like thunder outer China
        'crost the bay!

Tomlinson

Now Tomlinson gave up the ghost in his house in Berkeley
Square,
And a Spirit came to his bedside and gripped him by the
hair—
A Spirit gripped him by the hair and carried him far away,
Till he heard as the roar of a rain-fed ford the roar of the
Milky Way:
Till he heard the roar of the Milky Way die down and drone
and cease,
And they came to the Gate within the Wall where Peter holds
the keys.
"Stand up, stand up now, Tomlinson, and answer loud
and high
"The good that ye did for the sake of men or ever ye came
to die—
"The good that ye did for the sake of men in little earth so
lone!"
And the naked soul of Tomlinson grew white as a rain-
washed bone.
"O I have a friend on earth," he said, "that was my priest
and guide,
"And well would he answer all for me if he were by my side."
—"For that ye strove in neighbor-love it shall be written
fair,
"But now ye wait at Heaven's Gate and not in Berkeley
Square:

"Though we called your friend from his bed this night, he
could not speak for you,
"For the race is run by one and one and never by two and
two."
Then Tomlinson looked up and down, and little gain was
there,
For the naked stars grinned overhead, and he saw that his
soul was bare:
The Wind that blows between the Worlds, it cut him like a
knife,
And Tomlinson took up the tale and spoke of his good in
life.
"O this I have read in a book," he said, "and that was told
to me,
"And this I have thought that another man thought of a
Prince in Muscovy."
The good souls flocked like homing doves and bade him
clear the path,
And Peter twirled the jangling keys in weariness and wrath.
"Ye have read, ye have heard, ye have thought," he said,
"and the tale is yet to run:
"By the worth of the body that once ye had, give answer—
what ha' ye done?"
Then Tomlinson looked back and forth, and little good it
bore.
For the darkness stayed at his shoulder blade and Heaven's
Gate before:—
"O this I have felt, and this I have guessed, and this I have
heard men say,
"Get hence, get hence to the Lord of Wrong, for doom has
yet to run,
"And . . . the faith that ye share with Berkeley Square
uphold you, Tomlinson!"

The Spirit gripped him by the hair, and sun by sun they
 fell
Till they came to the belt of Naughty Stars that rim the
 mouth of Hell:
The first are red with pride and wrath, the next are white
 with pain,
But the third are black with clinkered sin that cannot burn
 again:
They may hold their path, they may leave their path, with
 never a soul to mark,
They may burn or freeze, but they must not cease in the
 Scorn of the Outer Dark.
The Wind that blows between the Worlds, it nipped him to
 the bone,
And he yearned to the flare of Hell-gate there as the light
 of his own hearth stone.
The Devil he sat behind the bars, where the desperate legions
 drew,
But he caught the hasting Tomlinson and would not let him
 through.

"Wot ye the price of good pit-coal that I must pay?" said
 he,
"That ye rank yoursel' so fit for Hell and ask no leave of
 me?
"I am all o'er-sib to Adam's breed that ye should give me
 scorn,
"For I strove with God for your First Father the day that
 he was born.

"Sit down, sit down upon the slag, and answer loud and
    high
"The harm that ye did to the Sons of Men or ever you came
    to die."
And Tomlinson looked up and up, and saw against the
    night
The belly of a tortured star blood-red in Hell-Mouth light;
And Tomlinson looked down and down, and saw beneath
    his feet
The frontlet of a tortured star milk-white in Hell-Mouth
    heat.
"O I had a love on earth," said he, "that kissed me to my
    fall,
"And if ye would call my love to me I know she would
    answer all."
—"All that ye did in love forbid it shall be written fair,
"But now ye wait at Hell-Mouth Gate and not in Berkeley
    Square:
"Though we whistled your love from her bed tonight, I trow
    she would not run,
"For the sin ye do by two and two ye must pay for one by
    one!"
The Wind that blows between the Worlds, it cut him like
    a knife,
And Tomlinson took up the tale and spoke of his sin in life:—
"Once I ha' laughed at the power of Love and twice at the
    grip of the Grave,
"And thrice I ha' patted my God on the head that men
    might call me brave."

The Devil he blew on a brandered soul and set it aside to
    cool:—
"Do ye think I would waste my good pit-coal on the hide
    of a brainsick fool?
"I see no worth in the hobnailed mirth or the jolthead jest
    ye did
"That I should waken my gentlemen that are sleeping three
    on a grid."
Then Tomlinson looked back and forth, and there was little
    grace,
For Hell-Gate filled the houseless Soul with the Fear of
    Naked Space.
"Nay, this I ha' heard," quo' Tomlinson, "and this was
    noised abroad,
"And this I ha' got from a Belgian book on the word of a
    dead French lord."
—"Ye ha' heard, ye ha' read, ye ha' got, good lack! and
    the tale begins afresh—
"Have ye sinned one sin for the pride o' the eye or the
    sinful lust of the flesh?"
Then Tomlinson he gripped the bars and yammered,
    "Let me in—
"For I mind that I borrowed my neighbor's wife to sin the
    deadly sin."
The Devil he grinned behind the bars, and banked the
    fires high:
"Did ye read of that sin in a book?" said he; and Tomlinson
    said, "Ay!"

The Devil he blew upon his nails, and the little devils ran,
And he said: "Go husk this whimpering thief that comes
    in the guise of a man:

"Winnow him out 'twixt star and star, and sieve his proper
     worth:
"There's sore decline in Adam's line if this be spawn of
     earth."
Empusa's crew, so naked-new they may not face the fire,
But weep that they bin too small to sin to the height of
     their desire,
Over the coal they chased the Soul, and racked it all abroad,
As children rifle a caddis-case or the raven's foolish hoard.
And back they came with the tattered Thing, as children
     after play,
And they said: "The soul that he got from God he has
     bartered clean away.
"We have threshed a stook of print and book, and winnowed
     a chattering wind
"And many a soul wherefrom he stole, but his we cannot
     find:
"We have handled him, we have dandled him, we have
     seared him to the bone,
"And sure if tooth and nail show truth he has no soul of
     his own."
The Devil he bowed his head on his breast and rumbled
     deep and low:—
"I'm all o'er-sib to Adam's breed that I should bid him go.
"Yet close we lie, and deep we lie, and if I gave him place,
"My gentlemen that are so proud would flout me to my
     face;
"They'd call my house a common stews and me a careless
     host,
"And—I would not anger my gentlemen for the sake of a
     shiftless ghost."

The Devil he looked at the mangled Soul that prayed to feel
    the flame;
And he thought of Holy Charity, but he thought of his own
    good name:—
"Now ye could haste my coal to waste, and sit ye down to fry:
"Did ye think of that theft for yourself?" said he; and
    Tomlinson said, "Ay!"

The Devil he blew an outward breath, for his heart was
    free from care:—
"Ye have scarce the soul of a louse," he said, "but the roots
    of sin are there,
"And for that sin ye should come in were I the lord alone.
"But sinful pride has rule inside—and mightier than my
    own.
"Honor and Wit, fore-damned they sit, to each his Priest
    and Whore:
"Nay, scarce I dare myself go there, and you they'd torture
    sore.
"Ye are neither spirit nor spirk," he said; "ye are neither
    book nor brute—
"Go, get ye back to the flesh again for the sake of Man's
    repute.
"I'm all o'ver-sib to Adam's breed that I should mock your
    pain,
"But look that ye win to worthier sin ere ye come back
    again.
"Get hence, the hearse is at your door—the grim black
    stallions wait—
"They bear your clay to place today. Speed, lest ye come
    too late!

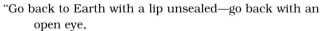

"Go back to Earth with a lip unsealed—go back with an
      open eye,

"And carry my word to the Sons of Men or ever ye come
      to die:

"That the sin they do by two and two they must pay for
      one by one—

"And . . . the God that ye took from a printed book be
      with you, Tomlinson!"

The Long Trail

There's a whisper down the field where the year
    has shot her yield,
  And the ricks stand gray to the sun,
Singing: "Over then, come over, for the bee has quit
    the clover,
  And your English summer's done."

You have heard the beat of the offshore wind,
And the thresh of the deep-sea rain;
You have heard the song—how long! how long?
Pull out on the trail again!

Ha' done with the Tents of Shem, dear lass,
We've seen the seasons through,
And it's time to turn on the old trail, our own trail,
    the out trail,
Pull out, pull out, on the Long Trail—the trail that
    is always new!

It's North you may run to the rime-ringed sun
  Or South to the blind Horn's hate;
Or East all the way into Mississippi Bay,
  Or West to the Golden Gate;

Where the blindest bluffs hold good, dear lass,
And the wildest tales are true,
And the men bulk big on the old trail, our own trail,
    the out trail,
And life runs large on the Long Trail—the trail that
    is always new.

The days are sick and cold, and the skies are gray and old,
    And the twice-breathed airs blow damp;
And I'd sell my tired soul for the bucking beam-sea roll
    Of a black Bilbao tramp;
        With her load-line over her hatch, dear lass,
        And a drunken Dago crew,
        And her nose held down on the old trail, our
            own trail, the out trail
        From Cadiz Bar on the Long Trail—the trail that
            is always new.

There be triple ways to take, of the eagle or the snake,
    Or the way of a man with a maid;
But the sweetest way to me is a ship's upon the sea
    In the heel of the North-East Trade.
        Can you hear the crash on her bows, dear lass,
        And the drum of the racing screw,
        As she ships it green on the old trail, our own trail,
            the out trail,
        As she lifts and 'scends on the Long Trail—the trail
            that is always new?

See the shaking funnels roar, with the Peter at the fore,
    And the fenders grind and heave,

And the derricks clack and grate, as the tackle hooks the
    crate,
        And the fall-rope whines through the sheave;
      It's "Gangplank up and in," dear lass,
      It's "Hawsers warp her through!"
      And it's "All clear aft" on the old trail, our own trail,
        the out trail,
      We're backing down on the Long Trail—the trail that
        is always new.

O the mutter overside, when the port-fog holds us tied,
    And the sirens hoot their dread!
When foot by foot we creep o'er the hueless viewless deep
    To the sob of the questing lead!
      It's down by the Lower Hope, dear lass,
      With the Gunfleet Sands in view,
      Till the Mouse swings green on the old trail, our own
        trail, the out trail,
      And the Gull Light lifts on the Long Trail—the trail
        that is always new.

O the blazing tropic night, when the wake's a welt of light
    That holds the hot sky tame,
And the steady forefoot snores through the planet-powdered
    floors
Where the scared whale flukes in flame!
      Her plates are scarred by the sun, dear lass,
      And her ropes are taut with the dew,
      For we're booming down on the old trail, our own
        trail, the out trail,
      We're sagging south on the Long Trail—the trail that
        is always new.

Then home, get her home, where the drunken rollers comb,
    And the shouting seas drive by,
And the engines stamp and ring, and the wet bows reel and
      swing,
    And the Southern Cross rides high!
        Yes, the old lost stars wheel back, dear lass,
        That blaze in the velvet blue.
        They're all old friends on the old trail, our own trail,
          the out trail,
        They're God's own guides on the Long Trail—the
        trail that is always new.

Fly forward, O my heart, from the Foreland to the Start—
    We're steaming all too slow,
And it's twenty thousand mile to our little lazy isle
    Where the trumpet orchids blow!
        You have heard the call of the offshore wind
        And the voice of the deep-sea rain;
        You have heard the song. How long—how long?
        Pull out on the trail again!

The Lord knows what we may find, dear lass,
And the Deuce knows what we may do—
But we're back once more on the old trail, our own trail,
      the out trail,
We're down, hull down, on the Long Trail—the trail
      that is always new!

When Earth's Last Picture is Painted

When Earth's last picture is painted and the tubes are
    twisted and dried,
When the oldest colors have faded, and the youngest critic
    has died,
We shall rest, and, faith, we shall need it—lie down for an
    eon or two,
Till the Master of All Good Workmen shall put us to work
    anew.

And those that were good shall be happy: they shall sit in a
    golden chair;
They shall splash at a ten-league canvas with brushes of
    comets' hair;
They shall find real saints to draw from—Magdalene, Peter,
    and Paul;
They shall work for an age at a sitting and never be tired
    at all!

And only the Master shall praise us, and only the Master
    shall blame;
And no one shall work for money, and no one shall work for
    fame,
But each for the joy of the working, and each, in his separate
    star,
Shall draw the Thing as he sees It for the God of Things as
    They are!

The Last Chantey

"And there was no more sea"

Thus said the Lord in the Vault above the Cherubim,
　　Calling to the Angels and the Souls in their degree:
　　　　"Lo! Earth has passed away
　　　　On the smoke of Judgment Day.
　　That Our word may be established shall We gather
　　　　up the sea?"

Loud sang the souls of the jolly, jolly mariners:
　　"Plague upon the hurricane that made us furl and flee!
　　　　But the war is done between us,
　　　　In the deep the Lord hath seen us—
　　Our bones we'll leave the barracout', and God may
　　　　sink the sea!"

Then said the soul of Judas that betrayed Him:
　　"Lord, hast Thou forgotten Thy covenant with me?
　　　　How once a year I go
　　　　To cool me on the floe?
　　And Ye take my day of mercy if Ye take away the sea!"

Then said the soul of the Angel of the Offshore Wind
　　(He that bits the thunder when the bull-mouthed
　　　　breakers flee):
　　　　"I have watch and ward to keep
　　　　O'er Thy wonders on the deep,
　　And Ye take mine honor from me if Ye take away
　　　　the sea!"

Loud sang the souls of the jolly, jolly mariners:
  "Nay, but we were angry, and a hasty folk are we!
    If we worked the ship together
    Till she foundered in foul weather,
  Are we babes that we should clamor for a vengeance
      on the sea?"

Then said the souls of the slaves that men threw overboard:
  "Kenneled in the picaroon a weary band were we;
    But Thy arm was strong to save,
    And it touched us on the wave,
  And we drowsed the long tides idle till Thy Trumpets
      tore the sea."

Then cried the soul of the stout Apostle Paul to God:
  "Once we frapped a ship, and she labored woundily.
    There were fourteen score of these,
    And they blessed Thee on their knees,
  When they learned Thy Grace and Glory under Malta
      by the sea!"

Loud sang the souls of the jolly, jolly mariners,
  Plucking at their harps, and they plucked unhandily:
    "Our thumbs are rough and tarred,
    And the tune is something hard—
  May we lift a Deepsea Chantey such as seamen use
      at sea?"

Then said the souls of the gentlemen-adventurers—
  Fettered wrist to bar all for red iniquity:
    "Ho, we revel in our chains
    O'er the sorrow that was Spain's;
  Heave or sink it, leave or drink it, we were masters
      of the sea!"

To the True Romance

Thy face is far from this our war,
Our call and counter-cry,
*   I shall not find Thee quick and kind,*
Nor know Thee till I die.
*   Enough for me in dreams to see*
And touch Thy garments' hem:
*   Thy feet have trod so near to God*
I may not follow them!

Through wantonness if men profess
They weary of Thy parts,
    E'en let them die at blasphemy
And perish with their arts;
    But we that love, but we that prove
Thine excellence august,
    While we adore, discover more—
Thee perfect, wise, and just.

Since spoken word Man's Spirit stirred
Beyond his belly-need,
    What is is Thine of fair design
In Thought and Craft and Deed;
    Each stroke aright of toil and fight,
That was and that shall be,
    And hope too high wherefore we die,
Has birth and worth in Thee.

Who holds by Thee hath Heaven in fee
To gild his dross thereby,
    And knowledge sure that he endure
A child until he die—
    For to make plain that man's disdain
Is but new Beauty's birth—
    For to possess in merriness
The joy of all the earth.

As Thou didst teach all lovers speech
And Life all mystery,
    So shalt Thou rule by every school
Till life and longing die,
    Who wast or yet the Lights were set,
A whisper in the Void,
    Who shalt be sung through planets young
When this is clean destroyed.

Beyond the bounds our staring rounds,
Across the pressing dark,
    The children wise of outer skies
Look hitherward and mark
    A light that shifts, a glare that drifts,
Rekindling thus and thus,
    Not all forlorn, for Thou hast borne
Strange tales to them of us.

Time hath no tide but must abide
The servant of Thy will;
    Tide hath no time, for to Thy rhyme
The ranging stars stand still—
    Regent of spheres that lock our fears
Our hopes invisible,
    Oh 'twas certes at Thy decrees
We fashioned Heaven and Hell!

Pure wisdom hath no certain path
That lacks Thy morning-eyne,
And captains bold by Thee controlled
Most like to Gods design.
Thou art the Voice to kingly boys
To lift them through the fight,
And Comfortress of Unsuccess,
To give the Dead good-night.

A veil to draw 'twixt God His Law
And Man's infirmity,
A shadow kind to dumb and blind
The shambles where we die;
A rule to trick th' arithmetic,
Too base, of leaguing odds—
The spur of trust, the curb of lust,
Thou handmaid of the Gods!

O Charity, all patiently
Abiding wrack and scaith!
O Faith that meets ten thousand cheats
Yet drops no jot of faith!
Devil and brute Thou dost transmute
To higher, lordlier show,
Who art in sooth that lovely Truth
The careless angels know!

Thy face is far from this our war,
Our call and counter cry,
I may not find Thee quick and kind,
Nor know Thee till I die.
Yet may I look with heart unshook
On blow brought home or missed—
Yet may I hear with equal ear
The clarions down the List;
Yet set my lance above mischance
And ride the barriere—
Oh, hit or miss how little 'tis,
My Lady is not there!

The Three-Decker

"The three-volume novel is extinct."

Full thirty foot she towered from waterline to rail.
It cost a watch to steer her, and a week to shorten sail;
But, spite all modern notions, I've found her first and
    best—
The only certain packet for the Islands of the Blest.

Fair held the breeze behind us—'twas warm with lovers'
    prayers.
We'd stolen wills for ballast and a crew of missing heirs.
They shipped as Able Bastards till the Wicked Nurse
    confessed,
And they worked the old three-decker to the Islands of
    the Blest.

By ways no gaze could follow, a course unspoiled of cook,
Per Fancy, fleetest in man, our titled berths we took
With maids of matchless beauty and parentage unguessed,
And a Church of England parson for the Islands of the
    Blest.

We asked no social questions—we pumped no hidden
    shame—
We never talked obstetrics when the Little Stranger came:
We left the Lord in Heaven, we left the fiends in Hell.
We weren't exactly Yussufs, but—Zuleika didn't tell.

No moral doubt assailed us, so when the port we neared,
The villain had his flogging at the gangway, and we
    cheered.
'Twas fiddle in the forc's'le—'twas garlands on the mast,
For everyone got married, and I went ashore at last.

I left 'em all in couples a-kissing on the decks.
I left the lovers loving and the parents signing checks,
In endless English comfort, by county folk caressed,
I left the old three-decker at the Islands of the Blest!

That route is barred to steamers: you'll never lift again
Our purple-painted headlands or the lordly keeps of
    Spain.
They're just beyond your skyline, howe'er so far you
    cruise
In a ram-you-damn-you liner with a brace of bucking
    screws.

Swing round your aching searchlight—'twill show no
    haven's peace.
Ay, blow your shrieking sirens at the deaf, gray-bearded
    seas!
Boom out the dripping oil-bags to skin the deep's unrest—
And you aren't one knot the nearer to the Islands of the
    Blest!

But when you're threshing, crippled, with broken bridge
    and rail,
At a drogue of dead convictions to hold you head to gale,
Calm as the Flying Dutchman, from truck to taffrail
    dressed,
You'll see the old three-decker for the Islands of the Blest.

You'll see her tiering canvas in sheeted silver spread;
You'll hear the long-drawn thunder 'neath her leaping
  figurehead;
While far, so far above you, her tall poop-lanterns shine
Unvexed by wind or weather like the candles round a
  shrine!

Hull down—hull down and under—she dwindles to a
  speck,
With noise of pleasant music and dancing on her deck.
All's well—all's well aboard her—she's left you far behind,
With a scent of old-world roses through the fog that ties
  you blind.

Her crew are babes or madmen? Her port is all to make?
You're manned by Truth and Science, and you steam for
  steaming's sake?
Well, tinker up your engines—you know your business
  best—
She's taking tired people to the Islands of the Blest!

The Miracles

I sent a message to my dear—
   A thousand leagues and more to Her—
The dumb sea-levels thrilled to hear,
   And Lost Atlantis bore to Her!

Behind my message hard I came,
   And nigh had found a grave for me;
But that I launched of steel and flame
   Did war against the wave for me.

Uprose the deep, in gale on gale,
   To bid me change my mind again—
He broke his teeth along my rail,
   And, roaring, swung behind again.

I stayed the sun at noon to tell
   My way across the waste of it;
I read the storm before it fell
   And made the better haste of it.

Afar I hailed the land at night—
   The towers I built had heard of me—
And, ere my rocket reached its height,
   Had flashed my Love the word of me.

Earth sold her chosen men of strength
   (They lived and strove and died for me)
To drive my road a nation's length,
   And toss the miles aside for me.

I snatched their toil to serve my needs—
   Too slow their fleetest flew for me.
I tired twenty smoking steeds,
   And bade them bait a new for me.

I sent the Lightnings forth to see
   Where hour by hour She waited me.
Among ten million one was She,
   And surely all men hated me!

Dawn ran to meet me at my goal—
   Ah, day no tongue shall tell again! . . .
And little folk of little soul
   Rose up to buy and sell again!

That Day

It got beyond all orders an' it got beyond all 'ope;
    It got to shammin' wounded an' retirin' from the 'alt.
'Ole companies was lookin' for the nearest road to slope;
    It were just a bloomin' knockout—an' our fault!

> *Now there ain't no chorus 'ere to give,*
>   *Nor there ain't no band to play;*
> *An' I wish I was dead 'fore I done what I did,*
>   *Or seen what I seed that day!*

We was sick o' bein' punished, an' we let 'em know it, too;
    An' a company-commander up an' 'it us with a sword,
An' someone shouted " 'Ook it!" an' it come to *sove-ki-poo*,
    An' we chucked our rifles from us—O my Gawd!

There was thirty dead an' wounded on the ground we
        wouldn't keep—
    No, there wasn't more than twenty when the front
        begun to go;
But, Christ! along the line o' flight they cut us up like
        sheep,
    An' that was all we gained by doin' so!

70

I 'eard the knives be'ind me, but I dursn't face my man,
  Nor I don't know where I went to, 'cause I didn't 'alt to
    see,
Till I 'eard a beggar squealin' out for quarter as 'e ran,
  An' I thought I knew the voice an'—it was me.

We was 'idin' under bedsteads more than 'arf a march
    away;
  We was lyin' up like rabbits all about the countryside;
An' the major cursed 'is Maker 'cause 'e lived to see that
    day,
  An' the colonel broke 'is sword acrost, an' cried.

We was rotten 'fore we started—we was never disci*plined;*
  We made it out a favor if an order was obeyed;
Yes, every little drummer 'ad 'is rights and wrongs to mind,
  So we had to pay for teachin'—an' we paid!

The papers 'id it 'andsome, but you know the Army knows;
  We was put to groomin' camels till the regiments
    withdrew,
An' they gave us each a medal for subduin' England's foes,
  An' I 'ope you like my song—because it's true!

  An' there ain't no chorus 'ere to give,
    Nor there ain't no band to play;
  But I wish I was dead 'fore I done what I did,
    Or seen what I seed that day!

The Vampire

A fool there was and he made his prayer
(Even as you and I!)
To a rag and a bone and a hank of hair
(We called her the woman who did not care)
But the fool he called her his lady fair—
(Even as you and I!)

Oh, the years we waste and the tears we waste
And the work of our head and hand
Belong to the woman who did not know
(And now we know that she never could know)
And did not understand!

A fool there was and his goods he spent
(Even as you and I!)
Honor and faith and a sure intent
(And it wasn't the least what the lady meant)
But a fool must follow his natural bent
(Even as you and I!)

Oh, the toil we lost and the spoil we lost
And the excellent things we planned
Belong to the woman who didn't know why
(And now we know that she never knew why)
And did not understand!

The fool was stripped to his foolish hide
(Even as you and I!)
Which she might have seen when she threw him aside—
(But it isn't on record the lady tried)
So some of him lived but the most of him died—
(Even as you and I!)

And it isn't the shame and it isn't the blame
That stings like a white-hot brand —
It's coming to know that she never knew why
(Seeing, at last, she could never know why)
And never could understand!

Recessional

God of our fathers, known of old,
    Lord of our far-flung battleline,
Beneath whose awful hand we hold
    Dominion over palm and pine—
Lord God of Hosts, be with us yet,
Lest we forget—lest we forget!

The tumult and the shouting dies;
    The captains and the kings depart:
Still stands Thine ancient sacrifice,
    An humble and a contrite heart.
Lord God of Hosts, be with us yet,
Lest we forget—lest we forget!

Far-called, our navies melt away;
    On dune and headland sinks the fire:
Lo, all our pomp of yesterday
    Is one with Nineveh and Tyre!
Judge of the Nations, spare us yet,
Lest we forget—lest we forget!

If, drunk with sight of power, we loose
    Wild tongues that have not Thee in awe,
Such boastings as the Gentiles use,
    Or lesser breeds without the Law—
Lord God of Hosts, be with us yet,
Lest we forget—lest we forget!

For heathen heart that puts her trust
  In reeking tube and iron shard,
All valiant dust that builds on dust,
  And guarding, calls not Thee to guard,
For frantic boast and foolish word—
Thy Mercy on Thy People, Lord!

The Explorer

"There's no sense in going further—it's the edge of cultivation,"
    So they said and, I believed it—broke my land and sowed
        my crop—
Built my barns and strung my fences in the little border
        station
    Tucked away below the foothills where the trails run out
        and stop.

Till a voice, as bad as Conscience, rang interminable changes
    On one everlasting Whisper day and night repeated—so:
"Something hidden. Go and find it. Go and look behind the
        Ranges—
    "Something lost behind the Ranges. Lost and waiting
        for you. Go!"

So I went worn out of patience; never told my nearest
        neighbors—
    Stole away with pack and ponies—left 'em drinking in
        the town;
And the faith that moveth mountains didn't seem to help
        my labors
    As I faced the sheer main-ranges, whipping up and
        leading down.

March by march I puzzled through 'em, turning flanks
    and dodging shoulders,
    Hurried on in hope of water, headed back for lack of
        grass;
Till I camped above the treeline—drifted snow and naked
    boulders—
    Felt free air astir to windward— knew I'd stumbled on
        the Pass.

'Thought to name it for the finder: but that night the
    Norther found me—
    Froze and killed the plains-bred ponies; so I called the
        camp Despair
(It's the Railway Cap today, though). Then my Whisper
    waked to hound me:—
    "Something lost behind the Ranges. Over yonder! Go
        you there!"

Then I knew, the while I doubted—knew His Hand was
    certain o'er me.
    Still—it might be self-delusion—scores of better men
    had died—
I could reach the township living, but . . . He knows what
    terrors tore me . . .
    But I didn't . . . but I didn't. I went down the other side.

Till the snow ran out in flowers, and the flowers turned to
    aloes,
    And the aloes sprung to thickets and a brimming stream
        ran by;
But the thickets dwined to thorn-scrub, and the water drained
    to shallows,
    And I dropped again on desert—blasted earth and blasting
        sky. . . .

I remember lighting fires; I remember sitting by them;
    I remember seeing faces, hearing voices through the
        smoke;
I remember they were fancy—for I threw a stone to try 'em.
    "Something lost behind the Ranges" was the only word
        they spoke.

I remember going crazy. I remember that I knew it
    When I heard myself hallooing to the funny folk I saw.
Very full of dreams that desert; but my two legs took me
        through it . . .
    And I used to watch 'em moving with the toes all black
    and raw.

But at last the country altered—White Man's country past
        disputing—
    Rolling grass and open timber, with a hint of hills behind—
There I found me food and water, and I lay a week recruiting,
    Got my strength and lost my nightmares. Then I entered
    on my find.

Thence I ran my first rough survey—chose my trees and
        blazed and ringed 'em—
    Week by week I pried and sampled—week by week my
    findings grew.
Saul he went to look for donkeys, and by God he found a
        Kingdom!
    But by God, who sent His Whisper, I had struck the
    worth of two!

Up along the hostile mountains, where the hair-poised
    snowslide shivers—
    Down and through the big fat marshes that the virgin
      ore-bed stains,
Till I heard the mile-wide mutterings of unimagined rivers
    And beyond the nameless timber saw illimitable plains!

Plotted sites of future cities, traced the easy grades between
    'em;
    Watch unharnessed rapids wasting fifty thousand head an
      hour;
Counted leagues of water frontage through the axe-ripe
    woods that screen 'em—
    Saw the plant to feed a people—up and waiting for the
      power!

Well I know who'll take the credit—all the clever chaps that
    followed—
    Came, a dozen men together—never knew my desert fears;
Tracked me by the camps I'd quitted, used the waterholes
    I'd hollowed.
    They'll go back and do the talking. *They'll* be called the
      Pioneers!

They will find my sites of townships—not the cities that I
    set there.
    They will rediscover rivers—not my rivers heard at night.
By my own old marks and bearings they will show me how
    to get there,
    By the lonely cairns I builded they will guide my feet
      aright.

Have I named one single river? Have I claimed one single
    acre?
  Have I kept one single nugget—(barring samples)? No,
    not I!
Because my price was paid me ten times over by my Maker.
  But you wouldn't understand it. You go up and occupy.

Ores you'll find there; wood and cattle; water transit sure
    and steady
  (That should keep the railway rates down), coal and iron
    at your doors.
God took care to hide that country till He judged His people
    ready,
  Then he chose me for His Whisper, and I've found it, and
    it's yours!

Yes, your "Never-never country"—yes, your "edge of cultivation"
  And no sense in "going further"—till I crossed the range
    to see.
God forgive me! No, *I* didn't. It's God's present to our nation.
  Anybody might have found it but—His Whisper came
    to Me!

Dirge of Dead Sisters

(For the nurses who died in the South African War)

Who recalls the twilight and the ranged tents in order
    (Violet peaks uplifted through the crystal evening air?)
And the clink of iron teacups and the piteous, noble
       laughter,
    And the faces of the Sisters with the dust upon their
       hair?

(Now and not hereafter, while the breath is in our nostrils,
    Now and not hereafter, ere the meaner years go by—
Let us now remember many honorable women,
    Such as bade us turn again when we were like to die.)

Who recalls the morning and the thunder through the
       foothills
    (Tufts of fleecy shrapnel strung along the empty plains?)
And the sun-scarred Red Cross coaches creeping guarded
       to the culvert,
    And the faces of the Sisters looking gravely from the
       trains?

(When the days were torment and the nights were clouded
       terror,
    When the Powers of Darkness had dominion on our
       soul—
When we fled consuming through the Seven Hells of fever,
    These put out their hands to us and healed and made
       us whole.)

Who recalls the midnight by the bridge's wrecked abutment
    (Autumn rain that rattled like a Maxim on the tin?)
And the lightning-dazzled levels and the streaming, straining
      wagons,
    And the faces of the Sisters as they bore the wounded in?

(Till the pain was merciful and stunned us into silence—
    When each nerve cried out on God that made the misused
      clay;
When the Body triumphed and the last poor shame departed—
    These abode our agonies and wiped the sweat away.)

Who recalls the noontide and the funerals through the market
    (Blanket-hidden bodies, flagless, followed by the flies?)
And the footsore firing party, and the dust and stench and
      staleness,
    And the faces of the Sisters and the glory in their eyes?

(Bold behind the battle, in the open camp all-hallowed,
    Patient, wise, and mirthful in the ringed and reeking town,
These endured unresting till they rested from their labors—
    Little wasted bodies, ah, so light to lower down!)

Yet their graves are scattered and their names are clean
      forgotten,
    Earth shall not remember, but the Waiting Angel knows
Them that died at Uitvlugt when the plague was on the city—
    Her that fell at Simon's Town in service on our foes.

Wherefore we they ransomed, while the breath is in our nostrils,
    Now and not hereafter, ere the meaner years go by,
Praise with love and worship many honorable women,
    Those that gave their lives for us when we were like to die!

The Broken Men

For things we never mention,
　For Art misunderstood—
For excellent intention
　That did not turn to good;
From ancient tales' renewing,
　From clouds we would not clear—
Beyond the Law's pursuing
　We fled, and settled here.

We took no tearful leaving,
　We bade no long goodbyes;
Men talked of crime and thieving,
　Men wrote of fraud and lies.
To save our injured feelings
　'Twas time and time to go—
Behind was dock and Dartmoor,
　Ahead lay Callao!

The widow and the orphan
　That pray for ten percent,
They clapped their trailers on us
　To spy the road we went.
They watched the foreign sailings
　(They scan the shipping still),
And that's your Christian people
　Returning good for ill!

God bless the thoughtful islands
    Where never warrants come;
God bless the just Republics
    That give a man a home,
That ask no foolish questions,
    But set him on his feet;
And save his wife and daughters
    From the workhouse and the street!

On church and square and market
    The noonday silence falls;
You'll hear the drowsy mutter
    Of the fountain in our halls.
Asleep amid the yuccas
    The city takes her ease—
Till twilight brings the land-wind
    To the clicking jalousies.

Day long the diamond weather,
    The high, unaltered blue—
The smell of goats and incense
    And the mule bells tinkling through.
Day long the warder ocean
    That keeps us from our kin,
And once a month our levee
    When the English mail comes in.

You'll find us up and waiting
    To treat you at the bar;
You'll find us less inclusive
    Than the average English are.
We'll meet you with a carriage,
    Too glad to show you round,
But—we do not lunch on steamers,
    For they are English ground.

We sail o' nights to England
    And join our smiling Boards;
Our wives go in with Viscounts
    And our daughters dance with Lords:
But behind our princely doings,
    And behind each coup we make,
We feel there's Something Waiting,
    And—we meet It when we wake.

Ah God! One sniff of England—
    To greet our flesh and blood—
To hear the hansoms slurring
    Once more through London mud!
Our towns of wasted honor—
    Our streets of lost delight!
How stands the old Lord Warden?
    Are Dover's cliffs still white?

The Settler

(South African War ended, May, 1902)

Here, where my fresh-turned furrows run,
   And the deep soil glistens red,
I will repair the wrong that was done
   To the living and the dead.
Here, where the senseless bullet fell,
   And the barren shrapnel burst,
I will plant a tree, I will dig a well,
   Against the heat and the thirst.

Here, in a large and a sunlit land,
   Where no wrong bites to the bone,
I will lay my hand in my neighbor's hand,
   And together we will atone
For the set folly and the red breach
   And the black waste of it all,
Giving and taking counsel each
   Over the cattle-kraal.

Here will we join against our foes—
   The hailstroke and the storm,
And the red and rustling cloud that blows
   The locust's mile-deep swarm;
Frost and murrain and floods let loose
   Shall launch us side by side
In the holy wars that have no truce
   'Twixt seed and harvest tide.

Earth, where we rode to slay or be slain,
    Our love shall redeem unto life;
We will gather and lead to her lips again
    The waters of ancient strife,
From the far and fiercely guarded streams
    And the pools where we lay in wait,
Till the corn cover our evil dreams
    And the young corn our hate.

And when we bring old fights to mind,
    We will not remember the sin—
If there be blood on his head of my kind,
    Or blood on my head of his kin—
For the ungrazed upland, the untilled lea
    Cry, and the fields forlorn:
"The dead must bury their dead, but ye—
    Ye serve an host unborn."

Bless then, our God, the new-yoked plow
    And the good beasts that draw,
And the bread we eat in the sweat of our brow
    According to Thy Law.
After us cometh a multitude—
    Prosper the work of our hands,
That we may feed with our land's food
    The folk of all our lands!

Here, in the waves and the troughs of the plains,
    Where the healing stillness lies,
And the vast, benignant sky restrains
    And the long days make wise—
Bless to our use the rain and the sun
    And the blind seed in its bed,
That we may repair the wrong that was done
    To the living and the dead!

Chant-Pagan

(English Irregular discharged)

Me that 'ave been what I've been,
Me that 'ave gone where I've gone,
Me that 'ave seen what I've seen—
   'Ow can I ever take on
With awful old England again,
An' 'ouses both sides of the street,
And 'edges two sides of the lane,
And the parson an' "gentry" between,
An' touchin' my 'at when we meet—
   Me that 'ave been what I've been?

Me that 'ave watched 'arf a world
'Eave up all shiny with dew,
Kopje on kop to the sun,
An' as soon as the mist let 'em through
Our 'elios winkin' like fun—
Three sides of a ninety-mile square,
Over valleys as big as a shire—
Are ye there? Are ye there? Are ye there?
An' then the blind drum of our fire . . .
An' I'm rollin' 'is lawns for the Squire,
              Me!

Me that 'ave rode through the dark
Forty mile, often, on end,
Along the Ma'ollisberg Range,
With only the stars for my mark
An' only the night for my friend,
An' things runnin' off as you pass,
An' things jumpin' up in the grass,
An' the silence, the shine an' the size
Of the 'igh, unexpressible skies. . . .
I am takin' some letters almost
As much as a mile, to the post,
An' "mind you come back with the change!"
                                        Me!

Me that saw Barberton took
When we dropped through the clouds on their 'ead,
An' they 'ove the guns over and fled—
Me that was through Di'mond 'Ill,
An' Pieters an' Springs an' Belfast—
From Dundee to Vereeniging all!
Me that stuck out to the last
(An' five bloomin' bars on my chest)—
I am doin' my Sunday-school best,
By the 'elp of the Squire an' 'is wife
(Not to mention the 'ousemaid an' cook),
To come in an' 'ands up an' be still,
An' honestly work for my bread,
My livin' in that state of life
To which it shall please God to call
                                        Me!

Me that 'ave followed my trade
In the place where the Lightnin's are made,
'Twixt the Rains and the Sun and the Moon;
Me that lay down an' got up
Three years an' the sky for my roof—
That 'ave ridden my 'unger an' thirst
Six thousand raw mile on the hoof,
With the Vaal and the Orange for cup,
An' the Brandwater Basin for dish,—
Oh! it's 'ard to be'ave as they wish,
(Too 'ard, an' a little too soon),
I'll 'ave to think over it first—
                                    Me!

I will arise an' get 'ence;—
I will trek South an' make sure
If it's only my fancy or not
That the sunshine of England is pale,
And the breezes of England are stale,
An' there's somethin' gone small with the lot;
For *I* know of a sun an' a wind,
An' some plains an' a mountain be'ind,
An' some graves by a barbwire fence;
An' a Dutchman I've fought 'oo might give
Me a job were I ever inclined,
To look in an' offsaddle an' live
Where there's neither a road nor a tree—
But only my Maker an' me,
And I think it will kill me or cure,
So I think I will go there an' see.
                                    Me!

The Second Voyage

We've sent our little cupids all ashore—
    They were frightened, they were tired, they were cold;
Our sails of silk and purple go to store,
    And we've cut away our mast of beaten gold
                (Foul weather!)
Oh 'tis hemp and singing pine for to stand against the brine,
    But Love he is our master as of old!

The sea has shorn our galleries away,
    The salt has soiled our gilding past remede;
Our paint is flaked and blistered by the spray,
    Our sides are half a fathom furred in weed
                (Foul weather!)
And the doves of Venus fled and the petrels came instead,
    But Love he was our master at our need.

'Was Youth would keep no vigil at the bow,
    'Was Pleasure at the helm too drunk to steer—
We've shipped three able quartermasters now,
    Men call them Custom, Reverence, and Fear
                (Foul weather!)
They are old and scarred and plain, but we'll run no risk again
    From any Port o' Paphos mutineer!

We seek no more the tempest for delight,
　　We skirt no more the indraught and the shoal—
We ask no more of any day or night
　　　Than to come with least adventure to our goal
　　　　　　(Foul weather!)
What we find we needs must brook, but we do not go to look,
　　Nor tempt the Lord our God that saved us whole!

Yet, caring so, not overmuch we care
　　To brace and trim for every foolish blast,
If the squall be pleased to sweep us unaware,
　　　He may bellow off to leeward like the last
　　　　　　(Foul weather!)
We will blame it on the deep (for the watch must have their
　　　sleep),
　　And Love can come and wake us when 'tis past.

Oh launch them down with music from the beach,
　　Oh warp them out with garlands from the quays—
Most resolute—a damsel unto each—
　　　New prows that seek the old Hesperides!
　　　　　　(Foul weather!)
Though we know the voyage is vain, yet we see our path again,
　　In the saffroned bridesails scenting all the seas!
　　　　　　(Foul weather!)

Piet

(Regular of the Line)

I do not love my Empire's foes,
   Nor call 'em angels; still,
What *is* the sense of 'atin' those
   'Oom you are paid to kill?
So, barrin' all that foreign lot
   Which only joined for spite,
Myself, I'd just as soon as not
   Respect the man I fight.
      Ah there, Piet!—'is trousies to 'is knees,
      'Is coattails lyin' level in the bullet-sprinkled breeze;
      'E does not lose 'is rifle an' 'e does not lose 'is seat,
      I've known a lot o' people ride a dam' sight worse than
         Piet!

I've 'eard 'im cryin' from the ground
   Like Abel's blood of old,
An' skirmished out to look, an' found
   The beggar nearly cold;
I've waited on till 'e was dead
   (Which couldn't 'elp 'im much),
But many grateful things 'e's said
   To me for doin' such.
      Ah there, Piet! whose time 'as come to die,
      'Is carcase past rebellion, but 'is eyes inquirin' why.
      Though dressed in stolen uniform with badge o' rank
         complete,
      I've known a lot o' fellers go a dam' sight worse than
         Piet.

An' when there wasn't aught to do
   But camp an' cattle-guards,
I've fought with 'im the 'ole day through
   At fifteen 'undred yards;
Long afternoons o' lyin' still,
   An' 'earin' as you lay
The bullets swish from 'ill to 'ill
   Like scythes among the 'ay.
      Ah there, Piet!—be'ind 'is stony kop,
      With 'is Boer bread an' biltong, an' 'is flask of awful Dop;
      'Is Mauser for amusement an' 'is pony for retreat,
      I've known a lot o' fellers shoot a dam' sight worse than
         Piet.

He's shoved 'is rifle 'neath my nose
   Before I'd time to think,
An' borrowed all my Sunday clo'es
   An' sent me 'ome in pink;
An I 'ave crept (Lord, 'ow I've crept!)
   On 'ands an' knees I've gone,
And spoored and floored and caught an' kept
   An' sent him to Ceylon!
      Ah there, Piet!—you've sold me many a pup,
      When week on week alternate it was you an' me " 'ands
        up!"
      But though I never made *you* walk man-naked in the 'eat,
      I've known a lot of fellows stalk a dam' sight worse than
         Piet.

From Plewman's to Marabastad,
   From Ookiep to De Aar,
Me an' my trusty friend 'ave 'ad,
   As you might say, a war;
But seein' what both parties done
   Before 'e owned defeat,
I ain't more proud of 'avin' won,
   Than I am pleased with Piet.
      Ah there, Piet!—picked up be'ind the drive!
      The wonder wasn't 'ow 'e fought, but 'ow 'e kep' alive,
      With nothin' in 'is belly, on 'is back, or to 'is feet—
      I've known a lot o' men behave a dam' sight worse than
         Piet.

No more I'll 'ear 'is rifle crack
   Along the block'ouse fence—
The beggar's on the peaceful tack,
   Regardless of expense.
For countin' what 'e eats an' draws,
   An' gifts an' loans as well,
'E's gettin' 'alf the Earth, because
   'E didn't give us 'Ell!
      Ah there, Piet! with your brand-new English plow;
      Your gratis tents an' cattle, an' your most ungrateful frow;
      You've made the British taxpayer rebuild your
         countryseat—
      I've known some pet battalions charge a dam' sight less
         than Piet!

Ford o' Kabul River

Kabul town's by Kabul river—
　　Blow the bugle, draw the sword—
There I lef' my mate forever,
　　Wet an' drippin' by the ford.
　　　　Ford, ford, ford o' Kabul river,
　　　　　Ford o' Kabul river in the dark!
　　　　There's the river up an' brimmin', an' there's 'arf
　　　　　　a squadron swimmin'
　　　　　'Cross the ford o' Kabul river in the dark.

Kabul town's a blasted place—
　　Blow the bugle, draw the sword—
'Strewth I sha'n't forget 'is face
　　Wet an' drippin' by the ford!
　　　　Ford, ford, ford o' Kabul river,
　　　　　Ford o' Kabul river in the dark!
　　　　Keep the crossing stakes beside you, an' they will
　　　　　　surely guide you
　　　　　'Cross the ford o' Kabul river in the dark.

Kabul town is sun and dust—
　　Blow the bugle, draw the sword—
I'd ha' sooner drownded fust
　　'Stead of 'im beside the ford.
　　　　Ford, ford, ford o' Kabul river,
　　　　　Ford o' Kabul river in the dark!

> You can 'ear the 'orses threshin', you can 'ear the
> men a-splashin',
> > 'Cross the ford o' Kabul river in the dark.

Kabul town was ours to take—
  Blow the bugle, draw the sword—
I'd ha' left it for 'is sake—
  'Im that left me by the ford.
    Ford, ford, ford o' Kabul river,
      Ford o' Kabul river in the dark!
    It's none so bloomin' dry there; ain't you never
      comin' nigh there,
      'Cross the ford o' Kabul river in the dark?

Kabul town 'll go to hell—
  Blow the bugle, draw the sword—
'Fore I see him 'live an' well—
  'Im the best beside the ford.
    Ford, ford, ford o' Kabul river,
      Ford o' Kabul river in the dark!
    God 'elp 'em if they blunder, for their boots 'll
      pull 'em under,
      By the ford o' Kabul river in the dark.

Turn your 'orse from Kabul town—
  Blow the bugle, draw the sword—
'Im an' 'arf my troop is down,
  Down and drownded by the ford.
    Ford, ford, ford o' Kabul river,
      Ford o' Kabul river in the dark!
    There's the river low an' fallin', but it ain't no
      use o' callin'
      'Cross the ford o' Kabul river in the dark.

The Files

(The Subeditor Speaks)

Files—
The Files—
Office Files!
Oblige me by referring to the files.
Every question man can raise,
Every phrase of every phase
Of that question is on record in the files—
(Threshed out threadbare—fought and finished in the files).
Ere the Universe at large
Was our new-tipped arrows' targe—
Ere we rediscovered Mammon and his wiles—
Faenza, gentle reader, spent her—five-and-twentieth leader
(You will find him, and some others, in the files).
Warn all future Robert Brownings and Carlyles,
It will interest them to hunt among the files,
Where unvisited, a-cold,
Lie the crowded years of old
In that Kensall-Green of greatness called the files
(In our newspaPère-la-Chaise the office files).
Where the dead men lay them down
Meekly sure of long renown,
And above them, sere and swift,
Packs the daily deepening drift
Of the all-recording, all-effacing files—
The obliterating, automatic files.

Count the mighty men who slung
Ink, Evangel, Sword, or Tongue
When Reform and you were young—
Made their boasts and spake according in the files—
(Hear the ghosts that wake applauding in the files!)
Trace each all-forgot career
From long primer through brevier
Unto Death, a para minion in the files
(Para minion—solid—bottom of the files). . . .
Some successful Kings and Queens adorn the files,
They were great, their views were leaded,
And their deaths were triple-headed,
So they catch the eye in running through the files
(Show as blazes in the mazes of the files);
For their "paramours and priests,"
And their gross, jackbooted feasts,
And their "epoch-marking actions" see the files.
Was it Bomba fled the blue Sicilian isles?
Was it Saffi, a professor
Once of Oxford, brought redress or
Garibaldi? Who remembers
Forty-odd-year old Septembers?—
Only sextons paid to dig among the files
(Such as I am, born and bred among the files).
You must hack through much deposit
Ere you know for sure who was it
Came to burial with such honor in the files
(Only seven seasons back beneath the files).
"Very great our loss and grievous—
"So our best and brightest leave us,
"And it ends the Age of Giants," say the files;
All the '60—'70—'80—'90 files
(The open-minded, opportunist files—
The easy "O King, live forever" files).

It is good to read a little in the files;
'Tis a sure and sovereign balm
Unto philosophic calm,
Yea, and philosophic doubt when Life beguiles.
When you know Success is Greatness,
When you marvel at your lateness
In apprehending facts so plain so Smiles
(Self-helpful, wholly strenuous Samuel Smiles)
When your Imp of Blind Desire
Bids you set the Thames afire,
You'll remember men have done so—in the files.
You'll have seen those flames transpire—in the files
(More than once that flood has run so—in the files).
When the Conchimarian horns
Of the reboantic Norns
Usher gentlemen and ladies
With new lights on Heaven and Hades,
Guaranteeing to Eternity
All yesterday's modernity;
When Brocken-specters made by
Someone's breath on ink parade by,
Very earnest and tremendous,
Let not shows of shows offend us.
When of everything we like we
Shout ecstatic—"*Quod ubique,*
"*Quod ab omnibus* means *semper!*"
Oh, my brother, keep your temper!
Light your pipe and take a look along the files!
You've a better chance to guess
At the meaning of Success
(Which is Greatness—*vide* press)
When you've seen it in perspective in the files!

The Gipsy Trail

The white moth to the closing bine,
  The bee to the opened clover,
And the gipsy blood to the gipsy blood
  Ever the wide world over.

Ever the wide world over, lass,
  Ever the trail held true,
Over the world and under the world,
  And back at the last to you.

Out of the dark of the gorgio camp,
  Out of the grime and the gray
(Morning waits at the end of the world),
  Gipsy, come away!

The wild boar to the sun-dried swamp,
  The red crane to her reed,
And the Romany lass to the Romany lad
  By the tie of a roving breed.

The pied snake to the rifted rock,
  The buck to the stony plain,
And the Romany lass to the Romany lad,
  And both to the road again.

Both to the road again, again!
  Out on a clean sea-track—
Follow the cross of the gipsy trail
  Over the world and back!

Follow the Romany patteran
   North where the blue bergs sail,
And the bows are gray with the frozen spray,
   And the masts are shod with mail.

Follow the Romany patteran
   Sheer to the Austral Light,
Where the besom of God is the wild South wind,
   Sweeping the sea-floors white.

Follow the Romany patteran
   West to the sinking sun,
Till the junk-sails lift through the houseless drift,
   And the east and the west are one.

Follow the Romany patteran
   East where the silence broods
By a purple wave on an opal beach
   In the hush of the Mahim woods.

"The wild hawk to the wind-swept sky,
   The deer to the wholesome wold,
And the heart of a man to the heart of a maid,
   As it was in the days of old."

The heart of a man to the heart of a maid—
   Light of my tents, be fleet.
Morning waits at the end of the world,
   And the world is all at our feet!

The Veterans

*(Written for the gathering of survivors of
the Indian Mutiny, Albert Hall, 1907)*

Today, across our fathers' graves,
    The astonished years reveal
The remnants of that deperate host
    Which cleansed our East with steel.

Hail and farewell! We greet you here,
    With tears that none will scorn—
O Keepers of the House of old,
    Or ever we were born!

One service more we dare to ask—
    Pray for us, heroes, pray,
That when Fate lays on us our task
    We do not shame the Day!

"Mary, Pity Women!"

You call yourself a man,
    For all you used to swear,
An' leave me, as you can,
    My certain shame to bear?
    I 'ear! You do not care—
You done the worst you know.
      I 'ate you, grinnin' there. . . .
Ah, Gawd, I love you so!

Nice while it lasted, an' now it is over—
Tear out your 'eart an' goodbye to your lover!
What's the use o' grievin', when the mother that bore you
(Mary, pity women!) knew it all before you?

It aren't no false alarm,
    The finish to your fun;
You—you 'ave brung the 'arm,
    An' I'm the ruined one;
    An' now you'll off an' run
With some new fool in tow.
      Your 'eart? You 'aven't none. . . .
Ah, Gawd, I love you so!

When a man is tired there is naught will bind 'im;
All 'e solemn promised 'e will shove be'ind 'im.
What's the good o' prayin' for The Wrath to strike 'im
(Mary, pity women!), when the rest are like 'im?

What 'ope for me or—it?
　　What's left for us to do?
I've walked with men a bit,
　　But this—but this is you.
　　So 'elp me Christ, it's true!
Where can I 'ide or go?
　　You coward through and through! . . .
Ah, Gawd, I love you so!

All the more you give 'em the less are they for givin'—
Love lies dead, an' you cannot kiss 'im livin'.
Down the road 'e led you there is no returnin'
(Mary, pity women!), but you're late 'in learnin'!

You'd like to treat me fair?
　　You can't, because we're pore?
We'd starve? What do I care!
　　We might, but *this* is shore!
　　I want the name—no more—
The name, and lines to show,
　　An' not to be an 'ore. . . .
Ah, Gawd, I love you so!

What's the good o' pleadin', when the mother that bore you
(Mary, pity women!) knew it all before you?
Sleep on 'is promises an' wake to your sorrow
(Mary, pity women!), for we sail tomorrow!

A Charm

Take of English earth as much
As either hand may rightly clutch.
In the taking of it breathe
Prayer for all who lie beneath.
Not the great nor well-bespoke,
But the mere uncounted folk
Of whose life and death is none
Report or lamentation.
    Lay that earth upon thy heart,
    And thy sickness shall depart!

It shall sweeten and make whole
Fevered breath and festered soul.
It shall mightily restrain
Over-busied hand and brain.
It shall ease thy mortal strife
'Gainst the immortal woe of life,
Till thyself, restored, shall prove
By what grace the Heavens do move.

Take of English flowers these—
Spring's full-facèd primroses,
Summer's wild wide-hearted rose,
Autumn's wallflower of the close,
And, thy darkness of illume,
Winter's bee-thronged ivy-bloom.

Seek and serve them where they bide
From Candlemas to Christmas-tide,
   For these simples, used aright,
   Can restore a failing sight.

These shall cleanse and purify
Webbed and inward-turning eye;
These shall show thee treasure hid
Thy familiar fields amid;
And reveal (which is thy need)
Every man a King indeed!

"For All We Have and Are"

For all we have and are,
For all our children's fate,
Stand up and take the war.
The Hun is at the gate!
Our world has passed away,
In wantonness o'erthrown.
There is nothing left today
But steel and fire and stone!
    Though all we knew depart,
    The old Commandments stand:—
    "In courage keep your heart,
    In strength lift up your hand."

Once more we hear the word
That sickened earth of old:—
"No law except the Sword
Unsheathed and uncontrolled."
Once more it knits mankind,
Once more the nations go
To meet and break and bind
A crazed and driven foe.

Comfort, content, delight,
The ages' slow-bought gain,
They shriveled in a night.
Only ourselves remain
To face the naked days
In silent fortitude,
Through perils and dismays
Renewed and re-renewed.
    Though all we made depart,
    The old Commandments stand:—
    "In patience keep your heart,
    In strength lift up your hand."

No easy hope or lies
Shall bring us to our goal,
But iron sacrifice
Of body, will, and soul.
There is but one task for all—
One life for each to give.
What stands if Freedom fall?
Who dies if England live?

My Boy Jack

"Have you news of my boy Jack?"
   Not this tide.
"When d'you think that he'll come back?"
   Not with this wind blowing, and this tide.

"Has anyone else had word of him?"
   Not this tide.
For what is sunk will hardly swim,
   Not with this wind blowing, and this tide.

"Oh, dear, what comfort can I find?"
   None this tide,
   Nor any tide,
Except he did not shame his kind—
   Not even with that wind blowing, and that tide.

Then hold your head up all the more,
   This tide,
   And every tide;
Because he was the son you bore,
   And gave to that wind blowing and that tide!

The Holy War

For here lay the excellent wisdom of him that built Mansoul, that the walls could never be broken down nor hurt by the most mighty adverse potentate unless the townsmen gave consent thereto.

Bunyan's HOLY WAR

A tinker out of Bedford,
A vagrant oft in quod,
A private under Fairfax,
A minister of God—
Two hundred years and thirty
Ere Armageddon came
His single hand portrayed it,
And Bunyan was his name

He mapped for those who follow,
The world in which we are—
"This famous town of Mansoul"
That takes the Holy War.
Her true and traitor people,
The Gates along her wall,
From Eye Gate unto Feel Gate,
John Bunyan showed them all.

All enemy divisions,
    Recruits of every class,
And highly screened positions
    For flame or poison gas;
The craft that we call modern,
    The crimes that we call new,
John Bunyan had 'em typed and filed
    In Sixteen Eighty-two.

Likewise the Lords of Looseness
    That hamper faith and works,
The Perseverance-Doubters,
    And Present-Comfort shirks,
With brittle intellectuals
    Who crack beneath a strain—
John Bunyan met that helpful set
    In Charles the Second's reign

Emmanuel's vanguard dying
    For right and not for rights,
My Lord Apollyon lying
    To the State-kept Stockholmites,
The Pope, the swithering Neutrals,
    The Kaiser and his Gott—
Their rôles, their goals, their naked souls—
    He knew and drew the lot.

Now he hath left his quarters,
　　In Bunhill Fields to lie,
The wisdom that he taught us
　　Is proven prophecy—
One watchword through our Armies,
　　One answer from our Lands:—
"No dealings with Diabolus
　　As long as Mansoul stands!"

A peddler from a hovel,
　　The lowest of the low—
The Father of the Novel,
　　Salvation's first Defoe—
Eight blinded generations
　　Ere Armageddon came,
He showed us how to meet it,
　　And Bunyan was his name!

Mesopotamia

They shall not return to us, the resolute, the young,
　The eager and wholehearted whom we gave:
But the men who left them thriftily to die in their own
　　dung,
　Shall they come with years and honor to the grave?

They shall not return to us, the strong men coldly slain
　In sight of help denied from day to day:
But the men who edged their agonies and chid them in
　　their pain,
　Are they too strong and wise to put away?

Our dead shall not return to us while Day and Night
　　divide—
　Never while the bars of sunset hold.
But the idle-minded overlings who quibbled while they
　　died,
　Shall they thrust for high employments as of old?

Shall we only threaten and be angry for an hour?
　When the storm is ended shall we find
How softly but how swiftly they have sidled back to
　　power
　By the favor and contrivance of their kind?

Even while they soothe us, while they promise large
    amends,
  Even while they make a show of fear,
Do they call upon their debtors, and take counsel with
    their friends,
  To confirm and reestablish each career?

Their lives cannot repay us—their death could not
    undo—
  The shame that they have laid upon our race.
But the slothfulness that wasted and the arrogance
    that slew,
  Shall we leave it unabated in its place?

The Benefactors

Ah! What avails the classic bent
And what the cultured word,
Against the undoctored incident
That actually occurred?

And what is Art whereto we press
Through paint and prose and rhyme—
When Nature in her nakedness
Defeats us every time?

It is not learning, grace nor gear,
Nor easy meat and drink,
But bitter pinch of pain and fear
That makes creation think.

When in this world's unpleasing youth
Our godlike race began,
The longest arm, the sharpest tooth,
Gave man control of man;

Till, bruised and bitten to the bone
And taught by pain and fear,
He learned to deal the far-off stone,
And poke the long, safe spear.

So tooth and nail were obsolete
As means against a foe,
Till, bored by uniform defeat,
Some genius built the bow.

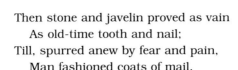

Then stone and javelin proved as vain
    As old-time tooth and nail;
Till, spurred anew by fear and pain,
    Man fashioned coats of mail.

Then was there safety for the rich
    And danger for the poor,
Till someone mixed a powder which
    Redressed the scale once more.

Helmet and armor disappeared
    With sword and bow and pike,
And, when the smoke of battle cleared,
    All men were armed alike. . . .

And when ten million such were slain
    To please one crazy king,
Man, schooled in bulk by fear and pain,
    Grew weary of the thing;

And at the very hour designed
    To enslave him past recall,
His tooth-stone-arrow-gun-shy mind
    Turned and abolished all.

All Power, each Tyrant, every Mob
    Whose head has grown too large,
Ends by destroying its own job
    And works its own discharge;

And Man, whose mere necessities
    Move all things from his path,
Trembles meanwhile at their decrees,
    And deprecates their wrath!

Epitaphs of the War

THE WONDER

Body and Spirit I surrendered whole
To harsh Instructors—and received a soul . . .
If mortal man could change me through and through
From all I was—what may The God not do?

HINDU SEPOY IN FRANCE

This man in his own country prayed we know not to what
 Powers.
We pray Them to reward him for his bravery in ours.

THE COWARD

I could not look on Death, which being known,
Men led me to him, blindfold and alone.

SHOCK

My name, my speech, my self I had forgot.
My wife and children came—I knew them not.
I died. My mother followed. At her call
And on her bosom I remembered all.

A GRAVE NEAR CAIRO

Gods of the Nile, should this stout fellow here
Get out—get out! He knows not shame nor fear.

PELICANS IN THE WILDERNESS
A Grave near Halfa

The blown sand heaps on me, that none may learn
 Where I am laid for whom my children grieve. . . .
O wings that beat at dawning, ye return
 Out of the desert to your young at eve!

THE FAVOR

Death favored me from the first, well knowing I could not
    endure
To wait on him day by day. He quitted my betters and
    came
Whistling over the fields, and, when he had made all sure,
    "Thy line is at end," he said, "but at least I have saved
    its name."

THE BEGINNER

On the first hour of my first day
    In the front trench I fell.
(Children in boxes at play
    Stand up to watch it well.)

A DEAD STATESMAN

I could not dig: I dared not rob:
There I lied to please the mob.
Now all my lies are proved untrue
And I must face the men I slew.
What tale shall serve me here among
Mine angry and defrauded young?

CONVOY ESCORT

I was a shepherd to fools
    Causelessly bold or afraid.
They would not abide by my rules.
    Yet they escaped. For I stayed.

UNKNOWN FEMALE CORPSE

Headless, lacking foot and hand,
Horrible I come to land.
I beseech all women's sons
Know I was a mother once.

RAPED AND REVENGED

One used and butchered me: another spied
Me broken—for which thing an hundred died.
So it was learned among the heathen hosts
How much a freeborn woman's favor costs.

SALONIKAN GRAVE

I have watched a thousand days
Push out and crawl into night
Slowly as tortoises.
Now I, too, follow these.
It is fever, and not the fight—
Time, not battle,—that slays.

THE BRIDEGROOM

Call me not false, beloved,
    If, from thy scarce-known breast
So little time removed,
    In other arms I rest.
For this more ancient bride,
    Whom coldly I embrace,
Was constant at my side
    Before I saw thy face.
Our marriage, often set—
    By miracle delayed—
At last is consummate,
    And cannot be unmade.
Live, then, whom Life shall cure,
    Almost, of Memory,
And leave us to endure
    Its immortality.